To our budding scientists

About this book
Kelly learns she will be staying home from school given the
COVID-19 pandemic. Her mom, a doctor, explains the science
behind the illness, viral transmission, social distancing, and
basic epidemiology to Kelly and her little brother Joey. Authors
Lauren Block MD MPH, a physician, and Adam Block PhD, a
public health professor, help parents explain scientific
principles behind coronavirus to their kids.

Kelly Stays Home: The Science of Coronavirus

Illustrated by Alex Brissenden

www.illus-bee.com

Blockstar Publishing

New York, USA

ISBN: 978-1-7349493-0-8 (ebook)

ISBN: 978-1-7349493-1-5 (soft cover)

ISBN: 978-1-7349493-2-2

Available at Amazon, Apple Books and on our website

www.kellystayshome.com

Email: coronaviruschildrensbook@gmail.com

Kelly is excited it's Friday. She has Friday free time at school, soccer in gym class, and it's her friend Eva's birthday. She puts on her red shirt for school spirit day, grabs a banana, and dashes out the door where she expects the school bus to be waiting. No bus! She glances at her watch. 8:15am; just when the bus arrives every day.

Kelly comes back in. "Mommy, where is the bus?"
"Kelly," says her mom, "I just got a phone call. We're going to have spirit day at home, because there's no school today."
"No school? On Friday? Woohoo, long weekend!" says Kelly.

"Wait, why?" asks Kelly, realizing this is not at all normal. She definitely didn't want to miss soccer and Eva's birthday.

"There's a reason you're not going to school and daddy isn't going to work at the office today," explains her mom. There is a new illness called coronavirus. It is spreading to people all over the world. It is a virus, just like a cold, or the flu. This virus is very contagious, which means easy to catch from other people. And it can make people sicker than the flu."

"Everyone is staying home because it is not safe to go to school or to the office. Mommy is going to the hospital tonight like normal to help take care of sick people, but you and Joey will stay safe at home with Daddy."

"Everyone's staying home? Even Cousin Clyde and Chloe in California?"

Mommy hugs Kelly. "This is happening all over the world, not just in our town, and not just in the United States. Families all over the world are staying home so we don't get sick. We won't go back to school on Monday, and probably not the next week. We could be home together for a long time."

Kelly asks, "Since there's no school, can we go to the playground with Eva?"
"Kelly, I am afraid we can't see our friends and we can't go to the playground for the same reason that school and work are closed. Eva will celebrate with her family, and we can call her later to say Happy Birthday. We also have a lot to do. We'll have school at home today. We just got some work from your teacher. And I'll need you to help me teach Joey the letters."

"The playgrounds are closed to make sure kids don't play and spread it to each other. The virus can even stay on the swings or park benches for days after people touch them. The only places open are 'essential' like the doctor's office, the pharmacy for medicine, buses and subways, and grocery stores where we buy food. The good part is that we'll have much more time to spend together as a family."

"Can we go visit Grandma and Grandpa? They're in our family," asks Kelly. "We can call them. Grandma and Grandpa are older so if they get coronavirus they can get very sick. Coronavirus can make it hard for people to breathe, which is why we must all do our part to reduce the spread through social distancing. Social distancing means we will stay away from crowded places and keep at least 6 feet distance from everyone else. 6 feet is about as tall as Daddy. This way, if anyone coughs or sneezes, their germs won't land on us. When we see our friends outside, it's fine to wave to them, but we can't high five or hug them like we normally do. It's important that you be a good role model for Joey. He will be looking to you to figure out what to do. Are you ready to do that?" Kelly smiles and shakes her head proudly.

"We can't do anything fun?" Joey says, stamping his foot.
"Sure, there are lots of fun things to do at home. After we're done with schoolwork, we can use this time to hike outside, learn to cook new things, play board games, and go for bike rides like a family. Remember, people are getting very sick, so we need to be grateful for what we have, like our health, our family, and a loving home with plenty of healthy food."
"And I'm grateful for dogs!" adds Joey.
"Right, and dogs," agrees Mommy.

"What is a virus?" asks Kelly as Joey climbs on his mother's lap.
"A virus tiny germ. It is so small that if you piled the virus on top of
each other it would take about a thousand to be the same thickness as
a piece of paper or a hair. It has little spikes on the outside that work
like glue and stick to everything like Velcro."

"Where did coronavirus come from?" asks Kelly.

"That's a great question," says Mommy. "Nobody knows for sure at this point. This is a new kind of coronavirus. Other types of coronavirus have been around for years and most cause people to get a cold. Scientists think this new strain may have come from a bat or an animal that looks like an anteater, called a pangolin. Since it is brand new, and right now there is no cure, the best thing is to stop the virus from spreading."

"The people in China and many other countries followed the rules to stay at home, wash hands, cover their sneezes, and avoid being too close to other people. With all that social distancing, the virus stopped spreading. This gives us lots of hope that we can also stop the virus from spreading here if we listen to the rules."

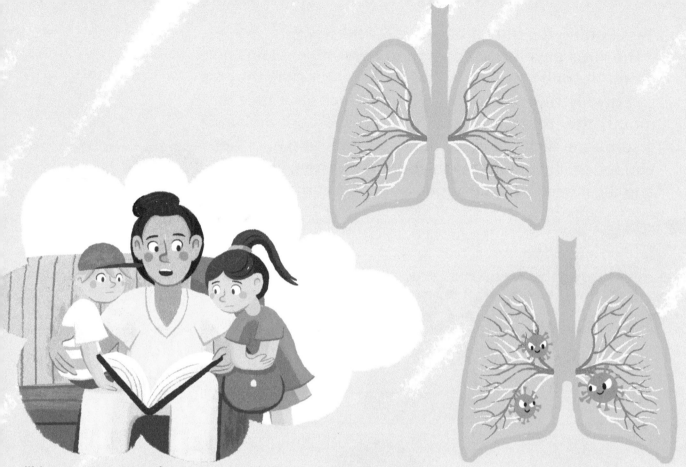

"How can something so small hurt us?" asks Kelly.

"Once the virus gets into your cells, the tiny pieces that make up your throat or your lungs, it causes them to stop doing their normal job bringing in oxygen and removing carbon dioxide from your body. Instead, all they do is produce more virus. People can then get sick with a disease called COVID-19, which means **CO**rona**VI**rus **D**isease first discovered in 20**19**."

"The virus typically goes into the lungs, which can cause them to stop working normally. That is why many people get a bad cough and trouble breathing. Some people with the virus get a fever as their body tries to fight the infection. Many people get better at home, but some people need to stay at the hospital where they are given extra oxygen to help them breathe. Sometimes, people even need a machine that breathes for them called a ventilator, to help their lungs recover."

"Am I going to I get coronavirus?" asks Kelly.
 "The virus travels from person to person," explains her mom. "If someone has it and touches your skin, they can give it to you, especially if you touch your face or mouth after touching them. You can even get the virus if someone with the virus touches something and then you touch it soon after with your hand. Then, like food and air, it can get in through your nose or mouth."

"So I won't eat it!" says Kelly, covering her mouth. Joey covers his ears.
"Joey, those are your ears, silly!" says her mom.
"The problem is the virus is so tiny, none of us can see it. And it's coated with little spikes which make it sticky, so it can stick to people's throats. The spikes are why it is call coronavirus, because they make it look like it is surrounded by a crown, or 'corona.'"

"How can just washing our hands help so much?" asks Kelly.
"Washing your hands is one thing we can all do to make sure that even if we come in contact with the virus, we will not get it," explains Mommy. "The virus is causing sickness worldwide, but it is destroyed by plain old soap. How you wash your hands makes a big difference. Washing effectively means washing your hands for 30 seconds, getting soap into a lather, rinsing, and drying your hands with a clean towel. This makes sure any coronavirus is washed away before we touch food, our face, or each other. If we sing 'Happy Birthday' twice, we'll make sure we're washing for 30 seconds."

After they wash hands, Kelly grabs a bowl and starts to pour cereal. She sneezes, "Achoo!" and the particles fly towards the box.

"The best way to keep it from spreading is to keep our germs to ourselves," explains Mommy. "Remember to sneeze into your elbow, not your hand or your food. That way, your hands and your food stay clean. This is another way we can prevent viruses from spreading."

"Sometimes I don't even know I'm going to cough or sneeze, it jus comes out of the sky," says Joey. "We can only do our best," replie Mommy. "So as another line of defense against getting sick, we wash our hands with soap and we disinfect anything we sneeze or cough on with bleach or alcohol-based cleaners. Remember, kids, we never drink these products. And we try to disinfect things that people touch a lot like phones, iPads, computers, and remote controls several times a day to make sure the virus doesn't jump from those objects to your hands. All that plus washing our hands with soap." "We're going to need a lot of soap," agrees Kelly.

"But how long do we need to stay home?" asks Kelly.

"We don't know yet, says Kelly's mom. "It will probably be several months. But even then things won't go back to normal immediately. We will probably go back to school, but we won't be able to go to concerts or baseball games for a while. The government is looking at how many people are sick in our area and will let us know when it's safe to go back to school and for Daddy to go back to his office."

"At the same time, doctors are testing new treatments, and scientists are working on a vaccine, or a shot, to prevent people from getting this illness to begin with."
"No shots!" yells Joey.
"None today," says their mom, smiling at Joey.

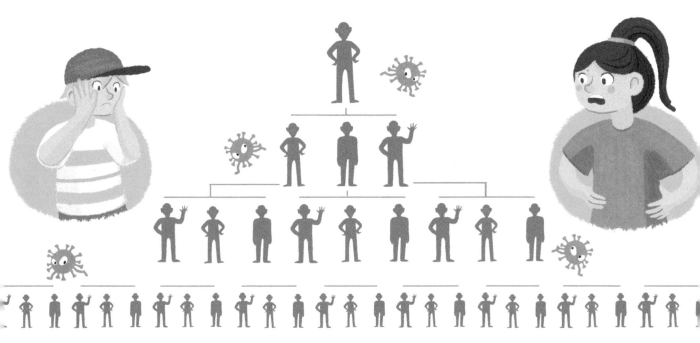

"But if everyone is staying home, how is the virus spreading?"

"Viruses are tricky little things. People can get it and feel totally fine for days before they get sick. This is called the 'incubation period' and can last two to fourteen days."

"Wait, what is the incubation period?" asks Kelly.

"This is when people have already caught it from someone else, but before they start feeling sick. So people can spread it to family and friends before knowing they are sick. This is how it spread so quickly. And some people get a very mild case so they do not even know they have it, but they can spread it as well. Now that thousands of people have it, it can continue to spread. That is why we need to all stay home. If one person spreads it to 3 people and each of them spreads to 3 people, then 9 new people will get infected. In two months, one person may spread it to over four million people.

"Wow!" says Kelly. "That a lot of people!"

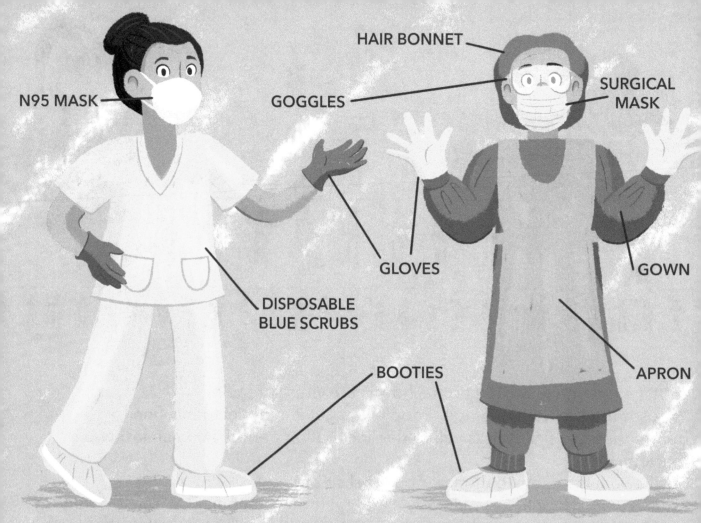

N95 MASK

HAIR BONNET

GOGGLES

SURGICAL MASK

GLOVES

GOWN

DISPOSABLE BLUE SCRUBS

BOOTIES

APRON

"If you are going to be around all the sick people, will you get sick, Mommy?" asks Kelly.

"Mommy works in the hospital, so all of the other health care workers and I are doing our best to help sick patients get better. Thankfully, I have lots of armor to help me stay safe while taking care of patients. Just like you, I wash my hands a lot. At the hospital I wear lots of protection - special scrubs, a gown, a mask, goggles, and gloves. I see patients when I need to, but other times I keep my distance to avoid spreading the infection. And I'm lucky to work with a group of special people who clean everything to make sure we all stay safe."

"Who else helps take care of sick people at the hospital?" asks Kelly.

"As a doctor, I work with a big group of caring people. Nurse practitioners and physician assistants help diagnose and treat patients, nurses check how patients are doing and give medicines and support to patients, pharmacists make sure patients get the right medicines, social workers help patients get the support they need at the hospital and when they leave, and lots of other dedicated people help too."

"What happens if I get coronavirus?" asks Kelly.
"Well, children your age rarely get very sick, thankfully. But if you or Joey come down with high fever, cough and tiredness, you'll tell me or your dad and we'll call your doctor. We'll make extra sure we take care of you and make sure nobody else gets sick, through a 'quarantine.' This means we'll stay inside for two weeks to make sure nobody else gets sick. And if you get worse, we'll go to the hospital where they can help you feel better. Almost all kids recover completely within a few weeks."

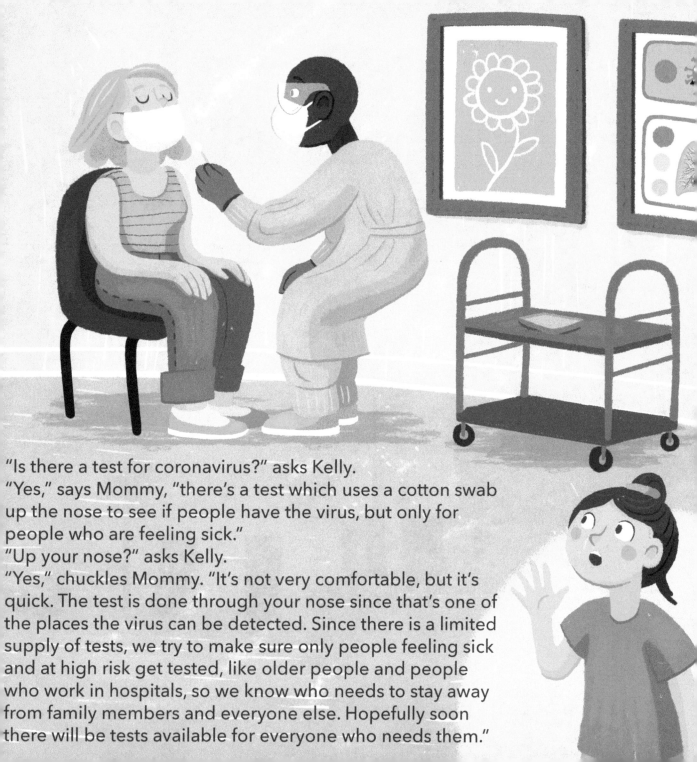

"Is there a test for coronavirus?" asks Kelly.

"Yes," says Mommy, "there's a test which uses a cotton swab up the nose to see if people have the virus, but only for people who are feeling sick."

"Up your nose?" asks Kelly.

"Yes," chuckles Mommy. "It's not very comfortable, but it's quick. The test is done through your nose since that's one of the places the virus can be detected. Since there is a limited supply of tests, we try to make sure only people feeling sick and at high risk get tested, like older people and people who work in hospitals, so we know who needs to stay away from family members and everyone else. Hopefully soon there will be tests available for everyone who needs them."

"Can medicine help?" asks Joey, pointing at the medicine cabinet.

"Many viruses like the common cold, the flu, and others have no real cure. Our immune system is our natural defense against viruses and other germs. Some other viruses like hepatitis are treated with medicines. We can cure lots of diseases, and one day scientists may figure out how to cure this one. People all over the world are working together to see which medicines will help people who are sick."

"At the same time, other scientists across the world are working on a vaccine to prevent everyone from getting this coronavirus. Scientists have basically ended diseases like polio, measles, and chicken pox this way. I had chicken pox when I was little, but you'll never get it because scientists invented the vaccine and your doctor gave it to you at your checkup."

"Is it like a cold where you can get it again next year?" asks Kelly.

"Since the virus is brand new, we are still learning about it. With many viruses, once you have it, you can never get it again because your immune system, which fights infections, is very smart. The cells in your immune system make a microscopic army of antibodies which remember the infection and how to stop it, so if you ever see the illness again, your body can fight it before it makes you sick. In fact, that is exactly how a vaccine, or a shot, works."

"I don't like shots!" says Joey.
"I know, Joey," says Mommy. "But vaccines are super important. Vaccines are the shots you get when you go to the doctor that keep you healthy. The doctor gives you pieces of the virus that teach your cells the secrets of how to fight it. When you get a tiny dose of dead or weakened virus, your body learns all about that virus, to make sure you never get it. Think about it like practicing baseball with a whiffle ball, so when the big game comes, you hit a home run with a real baseball."

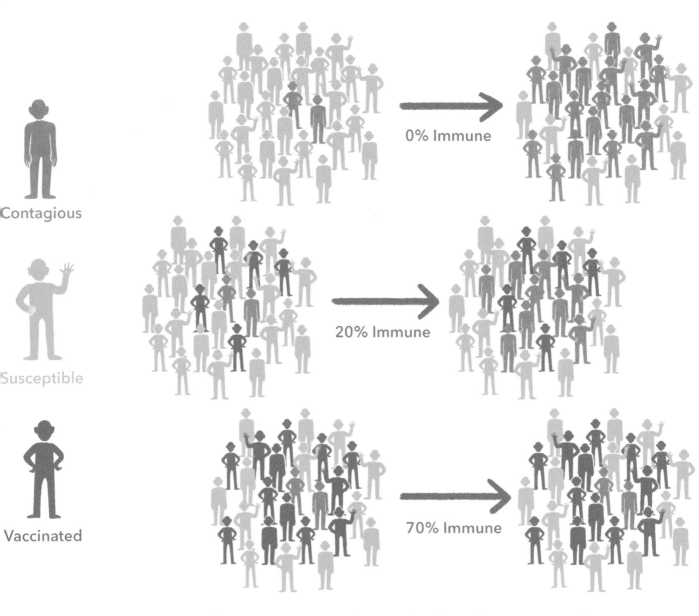

Contagious

Susceptible

Vaccinated

0% Immune

20% Immune

70% Immune

"What's more, if everyone around you also has the vaccine, that makes sure so little of the virus is circulating that even kids who don't get vaccinated, like kids who are born with medical problems, still get some benefit from the vaccines everyone else has. That's called 'herd immunity,' and helps keep everyone safe."

"Is there anything else we can do to help?" asks Kelly. "There's actually a lot we can do while we're at home. We will bring groceries to Grandma and Grandpa so they don't have to go out. We can donate to the local food pantry to help people who may not have enough healthy food to eat. We can reach out to people we know to help doctors and nurses get all the equipment to take care of patients. And we can write letters to ask the government to keep doing everything they can to make sure everyone stays safe at home until things are safe to go back to school and work."

"Well, for now we have lots to do here," thinks Kelly.
Ding! The cupcakes were done.
"There was bike riding, a crafts project, reading, and lunch. Maybe after lunch she'd work on a letter. "We'll have a great day today," says Kelly's mom. "We'll play soccer with Joey, talk with your friends, and do some science experiments later."
"So I can become a scientist one day?" asks Kelly.
"Right," says her mom, "so you can become a scientist and help keep people safe and healthy."

9 781734 949315